Justice

is a

Lady Lawyer

Attorney Erin M. Field

Justice is a Lady Lawyer

The Law Office of Erin M. Field
308 Enfield St, Enfield, CT 06082
(203) 418-8553
(860) 417-0814

Paperback
Expert

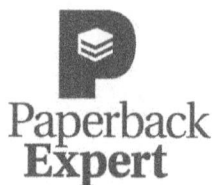

www.PaperbackExpert.com

Table of Contents

INTRODUCTION:

Falling on My Face

At the time, I had been a practicing attorney for about five years and worked for a foreclosure firm. All the attorneys were assigned to different courts and for this specific case, I was sent out to a court in Putnam, Connecticut. The judge overseeing my case was very serious and formal. A stickler for punctuality, he hated attorneys who were late or unprepared.

On this particular Monday, I was sitting in the second tier of the jury box alongside the other attorneys. When my case was called, I stood up and took a step forward. Standing in front of my chair, as I began to take the second step, my left heel got stuck in the strap of my pocket-book. Because it was wedged underneath the leg of the chair, I went flying.

I flew out of the jury box and landed flat on my face. I didn't land on my hands. I didn't land on my knees. I landed on my face. All in a matter of seconds, I was on the floor. Trying to figure out how I got there, half of the people in the courtroom were horrified, while the other half tried to stifle their laughter. After gaining my composure, I quickly stood right up, grabbed my file, and went up to present my case to the judge.

He never acknowledged the fall and I went on to present as if nothing had happened. I got through the rest of my cases and then I left. I remember that on the way back to my firm, I was in so much pain, I thought I had really done something to my face. Lucky for me, the carpeted floor cushioned my fall.

I've told that story to many people over the years and they can't help but picture the scene. There I was, a female attorney in a skirt, flying through the air in the courtroom – I mean, it's quite the image. But the reason why I'm telling you this story is because it was undoubtedly the most embarrassing moment I have ever had as a lawyer. I could not believe I had just done that–and I wished I hadn't. As funny as the story is, it just shows that no matter how careful you are, or how professional you are, you're going to make mistakes.

Everybody makes mistakes, but I try not to make mistakes when I'm representing somebody. I really strive to have an attitude like a surgeon. If a surgeon makes a mistake, a life is in danger. Although my job is not that important, If I DO make a mistake, somebody could be going to jail for a long time, getting a bad deal, or looking at a lawsuit. If I screw up something on their behalf, I could potentially ruin a life. So, I try to maintain a sense of perfectionism in my work because I love what I do and I love helping people.

The reason I became a lawyer was because of Perry Mason. When I was a kid, I used to watch a lot of Perry Mason reruns. At four or five years old I remember thinking, "Wow, this is so cool. Whatever this guy is doing, I don't know what he's doing, but this is what I want to do." I just always remembered that. I wanted to help people.

When I went through school, I figured that I would either become a lawyer or a journalist. When I realized that becoming a journalist was too difficult with years of low pay, and that I'd probably always be working for other people, I ultimately decided that lawyering was where I belonged. Fast forward to a couple years into my practice and I began to notice that I would meet these wicked smart women who had graduated from law school and passed the bar, but they didn't become lawyers. They would work for six months and quit, or never even get into the field at all.

I used to think, why does this happen? There are a lot of reasons for this, but I think the main reason is because law is a very intimidating field, and if you don't feel like this is what you're meant to be doing, you're going to feel out of place. There are young male attorneys who feel out of place too, but I think it's more prevalent with women attorneys.

Twenty-five years into my practice and I still meet young women who are quiet and soft-spoken. It's almost like they're saying, "Oh, I'm not here. You don't see me." And I don't understand it. Seeing women who are extremely insecure and unsure of themselves made me want to offer female attorneys the opportunity to get comfortable with feeling uncomfortable.

I think there are a lot of female attorneys out there who don't realize how excellent they could be because of little things that make them feel self-conscious. Ultimately, many just give up and go elsewhere. From my years of experience, I am hoping that women out there will read this book and follow my advice, because they can eventually get over these feelings of insecurity and intimidation. You can learn to be and become a successful lawyer.

Throughout this book, I talk about all the different ways and strategies of being a successful lawyer. Law school teaches you how to think like an attorney; this book will teach you how to

BE an attorney. Using strategies and tips that nobody teaches you in law school, you can learn how to be and become a successful attorney and have a great career.

Law is a very difficult field, but the truth is, nobody's going to kick you out or start screaming at you. Okay, so maybe they will once in a while, BUT they aren't going to slam the door in your face. So, I'm here to tell you that if you're a female, and a lawyer, you belong here. Own it, embrace it, make it yours.

Chapter 1.

Finding Your Area(s) of Practice

After graduating law school and passing the bar, young attorneys are tasked with the responsibility of starting their careers. As intimidating as it may seem, the key to finding success as a practicing attorney is finding your niche. My advice to young attorneys starting out straight out of law school is to find a job. Any job. Seize the opportunity to break into the field of law and discover your interests.

If you have an interest in criminal defense or prosecution, try to get a job in that area. If you like business and finance, look into the securities and exchange commission. Law is such a diverse field and there are so many areas of practice to choose from. Major areas of law include: Bankruptcy, Business (Corporate), Civil Rights, Criminal, Entertainment, Environmental, Family, Health, Immigration, Intellectual Property, International, Labor (Employment), Military, and Tax. As a lawyer, there is never any reason to be bored, even if you're doing something boring.

To survive in this business, you must have an idea of what you want to do. In the past, general practitioners could take on a variety of cases. They could do closings, set up trusts, estates, and even go to criminal court and defend less serious crimes. Although general practitioners could sustain their livelihood by taking on these cases, in the last 20 years, lawyers have had to say, "Okay. You know what. I'm giving up this part of my practice to focus on another part of my practice."

Up until recently, most lawyers had to be in practice for a long time before they got their name out there. The internet has changed that. Yes, people still need to see who you are and know that you have experience, but never wait until you land the "perfect" lawyer job to get into the business. Put yourself around other lawyers and pursue any opportunity that will bring you experience that will help build your career.

My point is this—just dive in. You have to dive in somewhere. Don't be afraid, because if you're not fearless as a lawyer, you're not going to make it. And if you do have fears, push them down, put them in the back seat. Put them anywhere other than your head because you have got to get out there.

Law is a highly cutthroat, competitive field that is full of ruthless individuals. You can't allow yourself to be intimidated by them. If this is what you really want to do with your life, then you need to find a way to do it. Don't let other people shatter your hopes and dreams of becoming a lawyer because you lack experience, whether straight out of law school or years into your practice.

The thing is, when you're in law school, they say, "Don't go to work for anybody. Just wait until you're out of law school." So, you don't. You get out of law school and get sort of stuck. As far as I'm concerned, that is a pretentious, elitist way of thinking. Before you make that commitment, you've got to be around the field and people to know if this is where you feel like you're going to belong or not. Don't be afraid to roll up your sleeves and get your hands dirty.

While I was working at a country club, the District Attorney from my city, who was a member there, said to me, "Somebody told me you're going to law school." I said, "Yeah, I am." He then said, "Well, do you want to come work for me?" I accepted his offer immediately because this was not an easy job to get. Usually to get into those jobs, you had to know somebody or have connections. Working there was a really great place for me to start because I feel like I got exposed to a lot of things while I was still in undergraduate school – things that most people don't get exposed to until they've been attorneys for five to ten years.

For many lawyers starting out, they end up working in an area of law that they don't like. Because of their experience, they believe that they haven't found their niche, and they give up. Too many lawyers give up before they've even started. They do it for a year and they go, "Oh. I'm not making any money. I'm quitting." So they go do something else that's completely unrelated. If you find yourself in an area of the law that you don't like, don't say, "Oh, I hate being a lawyer. I'm not doing this." Go find something else to do or find another area of practice, even if you have to break into it slowly.

Depending on what your market is, the experience is not always going to include getting out there, landing a great job, and making tons of money right off the bat. And you know what? I knew people who did get into those jobs right off the bat. They got out of law school, graduated top of their class, and went to work in New York City. One woman I knew quit her job after 10 months because she just couldn't keep up with that crazy work schedule. If you work for a firm in a place like New York City or even Boston, you're not going to have a life. You have to focus on your job and that's all you do. It's terribly difficult and some people just can't live that way.

So rather than giving up on the whole law thing altogether, just say, "Maybe I'm not meant to be a divorce attorney, maybe I should do real estate law." Maybe you'll say, "I can't be a bankruptcy lawyer because it's very technical and dry, maybe I could do environmental." You don't have to have advanced degrees either; you can be an environmental lawyer and not have a master's degree in environmental science.

You can get out of undergraduate school and say, "I'm going to law school and you know what, I love the environment." Once you've chosen your area, go for it. Don't let anyone talk you out of it. Give it at least two years before deciding whether you like it or not. It takes about five years to become a lawyer once you're in practice.

I could interview every single person who I went to law school with and I would get 200 different stories of how they got there and found their way or lost their way. But, every day, you have to get up and put your best foot forward and realize why you became a lawyer, remember why you are a lawyer, and why this means something to you. Yes, you can stop being a lawyer and get some other job, but take the chance.

You've got to find your own way and do what feels right to you at the time that you're doing it. If something starts to not feel right, you need to sit down and think about it and say, "What don't I like about where I am right now? Do I need to change it or do I need to just change my attitude?" You'll figure out what you need to do. The road-map for choosing your area of practice is to get up every day and do it.

And if you don't like your area of practice – pursue another one. If you don't love what you're doing – change it.

Chapter 2.

Gaining Visibility

After choosing an area of law, it is essential to gain professional visibility among other lawyers, judges, and others in the field. To do that, you've got to put yourself out there. Building from the last chapter, if you don't put yourself around other lawyers, you'll never become one.

> *Did you get that? Let me say it again.* IF YOU DON'T PUT YOURSELF AROUND OTHER LAWYERS AND STAY THERE, YOU'LL NEVER BECOME ONE.

What I mean by this is, don't work with other attorneys for two weeks and say, "Oh, gee. I don't like this." It takes several months, and even years. You've got to be in it every day. It has to be something that you are pursuing and that you don't want to stop pursuing. You need the job. You want the job. You want to keep doing what you're doing. There's a lot of people in this field who never really hit the bullseye because they never aimed for it.

The best way to gain visibility is to start working for someone else. When I was getting out of law school, there were no jobs.

I was involved with a guy who had a real-estate company and I started doing work with him. After that, I decided I had to do whatever I could to get some work as a lawyer. So, I started looking in newspapers. I found this one job as general counsel for a billboard company. I interviewed for it and got hired. After that, because the job was only temporary, I started looking at law firms and got a job at a pretty good law firm.

When I got that job, I was probably 29 or 30 years old, and I got my ass handed to me every day, either by a client, partner, or paralegal. Everyday there was somebody who handed my ass to me, and I stayed at that job for four years. When I left that job, I went to work for another firm that needed someone to set up an office in Connecticut.

I knew what to do because I had worked at a law firm for four years and had the background experience. I was still rusty on hiring people, but I took a class on how to hire people and then started doing it. I was working for somebody else and that job lasted about a year. Then I went out on my own and, since I'd been working in Connecticut for six years, I got calls the first day I opened my office.

To have a successful practice, use your contacts to your advantage. When breaking into any area of law, consider networking with other lawyers and working with them. To start, share office space, work with other attorneys, and learn from them. I can't stress enough the importance of putting yourself around other lawyers.

One of my friends from law school started his own practice. He went in with other lawyers and was able to get cases that way. It proved to be a successful way to build a practice and gain experience. I also know somebody else who tried to start her own practice right out of law school and had asked me if I could refer her to any lawyers. The reason why she didn't know any lawyers was because straight out of law school, she kept the same job she had always had, and had never put herself around other lawyers or gained any experience in law.

During law school, I quit all the jobs that I was doing and dealt with making 10 bucks an hour as a law clerk, but I was around lawyers all the time, and at the courthouse. I got exposed to the culture of attorneys. My friend, however, had no legal experience. She had always thought she would make a good lawyer. She was extremely intelligent and was on law review, but pursuing her own practice was not a good idea. I talked to another friend about her and he said to me, "A lawyer who's never worked at a firm or for another lawyer is like a loose cannon on the deck."

This is a powerful analogy because, if you think about it, the idea of a loose cannon on the deck of a ship is a compelling visual. What's happening? There's this cannon that is rolling around on a big ship, and it could go off at any minute. And if it goes off, it could blow a hole in the ship, injure people on board, and cause all kinds of damage. By saying this, he was bringing attention to what he, and I, have seen lawyers do – they didn't work for anybody in law school because law school tells you not to. I have seen this with mostly male attorneys, but female attorneys do it too.

My friend didn't do that. So, when she got out, she initially went to work for a solo attorney, another woman who had her own practice. Her practice was doing alright, but it wasn't terribly successful. She thought she could afford to take on an associate, but it didn't work out, and my friend ended up quitting that job after only about six months because she had missed out on several years of apprenticing or clerking for busy lawyers.

My point is, she went to law school for three years, was on law review, passed the bar, and gave up after six months. You have got to be kidding me. Unfortunately, I see a lot of women with the same story. She eventually went on to start her own firm and got her own office, but she ended up having to give it up after a couple of years. I think she really gave it her best shot, but she had already taken off three or four years between undergraduate and law school, and when you do that, you get on another track in life.

So, get a job. Whatever you can. Whatever it has to be. Get your name out there so people know who you are. The only way to do that is to hustle. If no one knows who you are, you cannot build a reputation and get more cases. I've worked for other attorneys. I did title searchers and research projects. I went to the courthouse in my city and I got myself out there. Prepare motions and do whatever you can. If you can't get a job in the field immediately, get a second job doing anything you can to keep money coming in. Once you gain visibility, you will get more referrals and more work. Be willing to put in the work and the time.

The best way to get experience in areas that you think that you are interested in is to contract yourself out as an independent contractor to other lawyers. Don't make them take you on as a full-time employee, because that's a lot of responsibility. Instead, to start, put up announcements. Say that you're a lawyer looking for clients. Advertise that you've graduated law school and you want experience. Offer support services and let it grow from there. It takes about five times of seeing your ad until someone will remember who you are.

When I had to get back into the field, I had to put myself back out there again. So, I got some business cards made up.

They're not that much money and ended up being a great way to network. I wasn't advertising myself as a lawyer, but as a side work assistant. I put them around the courthouse, and if anybody needed research, title searches, or anything, they could call me. I'll get it done for you at a reasonable price. And not only that, I was always visible. I was always there.

When I was doing legal work, I did it at the law library in the courthouse. When I would use the bathroom, I'd run into somebody. When I left the law library to go downstairs to get something to eat, I'd run into people. When I was in the hallways, I was talking to other attorneys all the time. I met people because I got out there and put myself where they were.

Simply put – gaining visibility means you've got to get over your shyness. You've got to get over the training that you don't have. Take a Dale Carnegie class, read some books on how to become more outgoing. It gets a lot easier once you start getting out there and doing it. Learn to relate to people, figure out who you're talking to and move on from there. The key to getting out there is knowing who you are and what you can offer.

If you don't land a job at first, it's best to break into the profession by building a network. Instead of venturing out on your own, work with other lawyers. Attorneys are usually looking for help. Approximately 75% of all attorneys are solo attorneys. Take cases from them to gain experience.

You don't have to have your own office. A good friend of mine went into practice with four other lawyers who were all established solo attorneys. He was 35 years old and knew that he had to just jump in and do it on his own. He left his corporate job that he could have kept for a long time and went to law school. At the end of law school, he went into business with the four other very established lawyers and did everything they asked him to do. He took all the cases they didn't want. One of the things he got handed to him turned out to be a very good personal injury case and he made $100,000. Six months out of law school and he had made 100 grand.

He used that money to advertise and get the best software equipment and other things he knew he would need as a lawyer. That's it – the daily grind of what you have to do. Make sure that you're out there and people see you. You have to be patient with yourself. Be persistent but be patient with yourself to learn what you need to learn and get good at what you're doing.

Day-to-day building–it takes years to grow a practice. I've known people who have worked in an area of law for 10 years and they never got good at it. Why? Because they were stuck in a job that they didn't like and never tried to leave, but just kept it. They've never really made it as a lawyer because they either picked the wrong field, were not well-versed in what they did, or never made the commitment to be successful.

When I left my last job working at a firm, I said to myself, "Well, I guess it's time for me to be on my own," because it didn't work out at the firm I had been working for. At this point in my career, I was in my late thirties and knew that I was going to be competing with kids that were 25, didn't have a life, didn't expect to have a life, and didn't care. That's was fine, because I knew that I had to start out on my own. So that's what I did. But this was after four years in one city, while I was still in undergraduate school. Then I went to law school and spent six years in another city working for other lawyers.

Gaining visibility happens one little piece at a time as you build your practice. There are people who I haven't seen in years, but they remember me. Not because I'm such a great lawyer, but because I got myself out there and did it every day, and I let people see me doing it every day. This is a people business. Whether it's corporate, government, or personal, you've got to be good with people, you have got to put yourself around those people, and some of those people have to be lawyers.

Growing your practice means becoming a lawyer that people know they can trust. To do this, you must always be 100% honest in your dealings with people. Whether it's a lawyer across the table, a judge, or one of your clients, tell the truth to everyone. If you don't, it doesn't take long to get a reputation as a liar. In my business, I know who the prosecutors think are liars. As a real-estate attorney, I knew who the liars were. I used to do a little bit of commercial litigation and there was this one man who I never forgot. Whenever he opened his mouth, I knew I couldn't trust a word he was saying because he was always lying.

If you are afraid to tell somebody something difficult, then you are not going to make it, because that is what lawyers do. You have to have a reputation of transparency and honesty, because this is not a career that's going to make you "feel good" all the time. We have to give news to people that they don't want to hear.

Loving what you do means loving helping people. The sense of helping somebody, even in the midst of a difficult situation, will make you a successful attorney. Aside from that, you have to work honestly, because if you don't, you will end up in jail. Not only will you end up without your practice anywhere, but you'll get disbarred and potentially serve time.

I know lawyers who have done it, but they didn't realize it was happening until it was too late. Why? Because they were ignoring it. They were ignoring the fact that they were only 30 years old and driving a Ferrari, and all they were was a lawyer. How come these 50-year old men don't have Ferraris? They've been doing it for twenty-five years, you've been doing it for five. You've got a Ferrari, he doesn't. Guess what? You're a liar. You're out here pretending to be somebody who got it on their own, when that's not true. Those people get caught – they always do.

As an attorney, you take your knowledge of the law and leverage that to help people in need. If you come across as trustworthy, you will be successful. Being honest does not mean perfection; it just means that you always represent yourself honestly, even if you don't have all the answers.

For example, sometimes people will ask me, "What exactly is the law on this?" If I know, I'll tell them; if I don't, I say, "Well, to be honest with you, I don't know exactly the law, but here's what I do know about this." And any holes that I left them with, I promise to fill in tomorrow. One thing I never do is make something up or lie. If you're not 100% sure on the law today, you can go home, open your computer, and find out in five minutes.

Clients are okay with that, and if they're not, they need to find a different lawyer. If they're looking for somebody that's just going to sugarcoat everything for them, then don't be that attorney. Let them go to another attorney, who just wants to tell them what they want to hear and take their money. Be honest, be upfront, use these strategies to boost your visibility and secure a professional identity.

Chapter 3.

Setting Up an Office

Although it's possible that you may start out sharing office space with other attorneys, setting up a solo office space should include some essentials. First, location is everything. When I started out on my own, I got a phone number, a yellow page listing, and found an office. If you're going to set up your own office, the best thing that you can do is drive around. Get in your car and drive around.

You never notice it until you start looking, but when I went to look for offices, I remember thinking, "I'm going to look in the paper and call up a realtor or two." Because I was looking for availabilities all the time, all of the sudden, these signs started jumping out at me, like street signs and signs in windows. They would usually say, office space available, followed by a phone number. Those signs are everywhere.

If you want to be in a location, neighborhood, city, or town, go to that area. Say, for example, that you want to be in the South end of Boston: drive through and stay on the main road. You don't want to be on a little side street where there's nothing else–you want to be around other businesses. Look out for office space near high-traffic areas like a bank, deli, or hair salon. For your first office, it doesn't have to be fancy or expensive. You don't have to have a beautiful office to convince people that you're a good lawyer. I've had offices that were presentable and nice enough, but I've never had a beautiful office. I've been in some lawyer offices and they're amazing, but you don't need it. All you're doing is passing on expensive rental costs to clients.

Until then, invest your money in an office space that you can afford and is in a great location. Drive around, pick a place, choose three to five numbers to call, and find out what the price is. If it's out of your price range, cross it off the list. Don't be discouraged–you WILL find something in your price range, in the neighborhood that you want to be in. You will. One important thing to look out for is parking. I found offices in the center of Hartford, but I didn't take them because the parking was terrible. One was $200 a month and another was $400. One of them was a beautiful office–I just couldn't believe it.

I remember my first thought was that there had to be something wrong with this building. Turns out, there was nothing wrong with the building, except the parking availability. They knew that once I walked around and started looking for the parking garages right around the area, I wasn't going to find any parking. Even if I could find parking for myself, how am I going to have parking for my clients that want to come see me, or that I want to come to my office? I don't always want to go to my clients. I am willing to do that, but I don't always want to have to do that.

Aside from parking, any attorney, especially if you're a female attorney, has to be aware of the area surrounding the office. If the outside looks scary to you, it's going to look scary to every other female that comes out there, and probably half of the men. Not every man wants to get out of his car in the middle of a questionable area and walk three blocks to your office. There was a great office I wanted to rent—the building was beautiful—but the only parking was in this scary parking garage, and there was no street parking. Even if there was street parking, believe me, when you're in the middle of a city, finding parking is a big deal.

So, when picking a location, make sure that not only does the office look somewhat welcoming to someone, but that you're also not in a neighborhood where you really shouldn't be. When I was working at my very first law firm, people constantly complained about the location. They hated it, and the partners just didn't care. I cared, and I thought it was ridiculous. Your office is representative of your business. It doesn't have to look like a palace, it just has to look presentable, that's it. If things need to be repaired, repair them. Do what you can to improve the outside appearance.

There's a bunch of empty first floor office buildings in Hartford, Connecticut. They have been this way for ten years now, and people are slowly leaving because of the conditions of these offices. If the building has broken windows downstairs and you're in the second floor of the building, it's not a good idea.

When people pull up outside of your building and they see a big sign out front that says, "First floor available" and they see that your office is above that, it raises questions, and they will begin to wonder about the vacancy. If you're in a prime location and your building has a lot of vacancy, you don't want to be there. Even if it's cheap, you don't want to be in that location. Pay the extra little bit of money and get a decent location so that both men and women will want to come to your office.

To sum it up, an ideal office location should be easy to find, have ample parking, and be located in a safe, visible area. After you select a place, find out the financial details. I have never once signed a lease to rent an office. I have been on my own since 2004 and have never leased an office. However, I wouldn't necessarily say that's a good thing. If you find a great office with a one-year lease, and you're pretty sure you can make a go of it there, go ahead and sign it. Otherwise, my advice is to avoid getting roped into a long lease.

Make your decision cautiously because you have to remember, as a commercial tenant, you don't have any rights. If you are late one month's rent, the landlord can literally lock your doors after he or she sends you a three-day notice. If you don't get that money to them, they can shut down your office and sell your furniture. Although that's a worst-case scenario, you don't want to rent from a big commercial landlord if you can avoid it.

For attorneys, it's better to find smaller places, because you don't know what's going to change in that neighborhood over the next six months. Things can happen that will make you not want to be there, and I know this because I have had this happen. By getting tied up into a long lease, you could end up owing a lot of money, and it could end up putting you under.

Now that you've found a place, you can focus on the inside. As a place of business, an office should feature standard amenities such as a desk, computer, internet access, phone, filing cabinets, and basic office supplies. As I said, when you're starting out, you should find ways to save money where you can. When you're opening your own office, your first office, there is no need to buy brand new furniture. Brand new furniture is crazy expensive and, in my opinion, it is one of the biggest scams ever. My advice is to buy used furniture. Go to a used office furniture store, or look around in local ads in the newspaper.

There was one time when I went to look at an office, and I told the guy renting the building that I didn't like the set-up, as it had a cubicle-like layout which was not what I was looking for. As a lawyer, I needed to have my own space where no one could hear me talking so I could ensure confidentiality with my clients. He understood that the space wouldn't work for me, but pointed at some furniture in the room and said it was for sale.

As we were talking, he started telling me the prices and I couldn't believe it. He told me that the guy selling it was asking $200, so right then and there I pulled out my checkbook and wrote him a check for $200. I told him I'd be sending somebody to pick up the furniture within the next couple days. He agreed, and that's how I got my first office furniture. It was just what I was looking for, and I realized right then that you have got to be out there interacting with people. You'll end up going to places and finding ways to make it happen for you.

Another thing I did when I got my first office was have a guy build me a table. I knew that I was going to need a closing table, and it needed to be a certain size. Getting custom made furniture is not that expensive, especially if it's a simple piece. I ended up paying about $150 for it and it worked really well. After a while, I moved offices, and decided that at my new office I didn't want a square closing table, but a round one. I ended up giving that table away, but I called the same guy again and he built me another table, this time a round one, for my new office. I had that table for a very long time, and it was a really good purchase.

Keep in mind that office furniture typically lasts a long time. It's not going to get beat up unless you have five-year olds over at your office running around. For the most part, it's going to last.

You can always find really good deals if you look, so don't buy expensive new furniture–it's not necessary. Just make sure that the office furniture that you do buy is appropriate for the office that you're renting. You really need the office first. Don't just buy furniture and hope that it fits in the office – get the office first.

Considering the size of the space is essential. My first office was 400 square-feet and I made sure that the furniture was appropriate for that space. It's important that the space feels comfy and not cramped. An example of this happened during a closing. I was working at a firm during the time and I go to this closing where I didn't know the other lawyer. A lot of the other firms did not like our firm because we were part of a network that the partners bought into, although I personally didn't buy into it and I wasn't a partner. The law office I worked for was in this network and being a part of it was supposed to make things easy and streamlined for foreclosures for the banks. For this reason, a lot of the law firms disliked our office and took it out on the associates, which was me.

Upon entering his office, the first thing I notice is how small it is. I can't believe I'm getting stuck in this office, because the furniture is really huge, and the space cannot accommodate it. The lawyer gets up from the end of the table, and as he stands up, he has to walk out away from the end of the table so that I can walk in. As he moves to make room for me, I sit down in the cramped little corner that he directs me to. As I'm sitting next to him, he immediately begins to get angry. He's upset about this closing, upset that Freddie Mac had not made any concessions, and he was expecting to receive concessions.

He's expecting me to solve this problem and you've got to understand that at the time, when you work for Freddie Mac*, and I'm sure it remains the same today, it's a take it or leave it deal. I politely tell him that I'm sorry, but this is the deal. This is the HUD one that they approved, and this is the deal. He was extremely angry. He started to yell and pound the table – as I'm sitting next to him. Now I'm getting a little scared because I don't like how this is going and now I'm stuck in this corner while everyone else in the room is on the same side, except me.

The realtors are just looking at their hands while I'm trying to tell him that I'm sorry he doesn't like this deal, but this is what your clients agreed to. We didn't change anything, this was the deal with Freddie Mac, take it or don't. He continues to rip into me, berating my firm and me. I wasn't going to take this. So I decided I had to do something.

I was probably 30 or 31 years old at the time, but I asked him to get up because I was going to leave. He said, "You're not going anywhere. I don't know who you think you are, but you're not going anywhere." I said, "No, I'm leaving. You need to get up, I'm leaving." He kept telling me he wasn't going to move, because I wasn't going anywhere. So, I stood up as he was still sitting down and said, "You better move now." Mind you, I was still being very polite, very calm, and nobody was saying anything. Nobody else said a word. They were all just sitting there waiting to see what was going to happen.

He finally stood up, but he was blocking me and he wouldn't let me go. He's not putting his hands on me, but he's not letting me leave. In that moment, I turned into a lioness. I come from a big family and I'm not afraid to use my voice, so I just growled at him to get out of my way. Through clenched teeth I'm growling at him to move, not screaming or shouting, just using a very serious tone.

He finally moved out of my way, but I was extremely shaken by it. I remember going back to my office, so upset because I could not believe that I had been treated that way by another attorney. I went to my boss, handed him the file and told him that I was not going back there. I partly believe he behaved that way because I was a female attorney, a lot younger than him, and to also put on a show for his clients, but I did not tolerate it. I've never taken that behavior from somebody as a lawyer, and you don't have to. The point is, if that guy had actual office furniture that was appropriate for the office, I would have been able to easily leave. No one should ever feel trapped in your office.

To avoid making an office space appear too big or too small, make sure that the furniture also complements the rest of the things in the room. You want to put up some things in your office that people can talk about. I don't necessarily think that you need to put your law school diploma on the wall, but put some conversation starters around the room. Find an interesting piece of artwork that you picked up from an estate sale, or a unique painting. I always had pictures around my office so that people could ask about them.

Having a clean office space is also important. Not spotlessly, but before you leave every day, pick up your office. Don't leave piles of paper and files scattered about. It's confidential information, and it makes a bad impression on people coming into your office. Every person that has ever set foot in my office said, "Wow, this is so clean. I thought lawyers were slobs." Some of us are, some of us aren't. Pay attention to the details—it will benefit you in the long run.

The entire process of setting up an office can take place in the span of a week. First you find the office, then you make the down payment, select a move in date, get furniture, and that's it, you're ready. All of this assumes that you are either setting up an office alone, or with other attorneys. Depending on how many lawyers you're going to be working with, if it's just you and somebody else, then just get furniture that works for the both of you. There is no need to have a computer network set up unless you're going to be sharing files. You can each have your own computer and individual systems.

As you begin to finalize everything, it is important to remember that each lawyer needs to know what their state requires of them. You need to set up the proper bank accounts that are required by the state that you're licensed in. You usually have to have these accounts located in that state, and depending on state requirements, there may be additional requirements. For example, in Connecticut, we are required to have an IOLTA. In addition to that, we also have to have an operating account, and depending on the type of work you do, you might need another separate client funds account. You must be diligent with your money and make sure that you are not commingling funds, as it can lead to serious trouble with respect to your license.

Commingling funds happens when you have not earned a specific amount of money yet, but you have it in the account that you would put it in, as if you had earned it. Or, this happens when you have earned a specific amount, but you keep it in the account that it needs to come out of. Simply, commingling funds is what happens when lawyers mix their money with their clients' money, which is not allowed. If you don't have the proper accounts, you're going to find yourself in trouble with the BAR in your state, and possibly with the IRS.

The IRS targets lawyers, doctors, and small-business owners. Because of this, it's important to hire someone, part time, to handle your finances. They don't even have to work in your office. I don't have a staff, but I have a bookkeeper that I send statements to every month. I send receipts, and he knows which statements are personal or business expenses. He knows which cards go with each account, and I just let him handle it, because a lawyer who thinks they can do their own bookkeeping and accounting is just asking for trouble. I also have a Certified Public Accountant (CPA) to do my taxes to make sure that everything is in order. I cannot stress enough the importance of making sure that your finances are in order.

Another important aspect of setting up a practice is liability insurance. You have to have it. If you don't, you're just an accident waiting to happen. For lawyers, liability insurance functions the same way it does for physicians. A physician has liability insurance because they are giving patients advice, they are writing prescriptions, etc. Lawyers also need liability insurance, because if somebody thinks that you misrepresented them in some way, and they decide to sue you, you're protected. If you don't have liability insurance, you could be on the hook for it, and if you lose that lawsuit, your firm could be shut down.

Liability insurance is your safeguard just in case somebody thinks they have a reason to sue you and decide to come after you. A few years ago, I represented some clients who ended up suing me. I won the suit, but if I had not had liability insurance it would have been difficult. I do not advise representing yourself—it is a huge mistake. If you have liability insurance, the insurance company handles everything. They hire the lawyer for you and make sure that you're well protected. The insurance company I used let me pick my attorney and the entire process was handled very well. All of these things are important when setting up an office. Having a successful practice depends on it.

Chapter 4.

Dressing Like a Lawyer

When starting out as a young attorney, or if you're a practicing attorney of any age, you are always having to prove your credibility as a lawyer. As much as I hate to admit this, when you're meeting clients, especially as a female, they are likely judging you from head to toe. The reason why you have to have present yourself a certain way is because you're a female attorney. You have to dress in accordance with the expectations of the legal profession. You always want people to partly view you by the way you dress, and they should be able to tell that you take your job seriously.

As you advance in your career, you can become more relaxed and wear casual clothing when visiting with clients, but you must ALWAYS maintain the appearance of professionalism. When it comes to the rules of attire, they are different for men and women. The truth is, men are usually restricted to a suit, tie, and nice shoes. That is their dress code. For women, the rules are different. You are likely not going to wear a suit and tie, but you can dress modestly and appropriately while maintaining your femininity.

I believe that a lawyer who does not go to court should still dress like one who does. Meaning, even if you're not due in court, dress as if you were, put care into your appearance. Over the years, I have come across many female attorneys who were not dressed appropriately in a professional setting. I remember one woman showed up to court in a skin-tight leopard skirt and stiletto high-heels. I was shocked. Not only was this completely inappropriate for the courtroom, but it was also very distracting. To avoid looking too sexy or casual, avoid plunging necklines, sleeveless blouses, and clingy, tight clothing. This does not translate well, and no one will take you seriously.

The main thing to remember is modesty. I always wear a jacket and firmly believe that all lawyers should always wear a jacket—not a sweater, not a vest, a jacket. You can pair jackets with a variety of things, like if you wear a pantsuit and find a coordinating blouse to match. Select a feminine silhouette that features slight shoulder pads that elongate your stature. Bulky pads will make your shoulders appear broad and masculine—you don't want to look like a man. When choosing colors and patterns, avoid loud patterns such as flowers and stripes and select solid colors that can be paired with a variety of different combinations.

You can also choose to wear a dress, though the only female attorneys I see that can get away with that have always been prosecutors. Even still, they make sure they always look polished. The dress is always a modest length, either at the knee or slightly below. Aside from clothing, you always want to make sure you have appropriate shoes; wearing flip flops to court is not acceptable. Find a low heel that is comfortable enough to walk in but not too casual. Don't worry about breaking the bank, as you can find appropriate clothing on a budget. I bought my first suits for

$10 a piece at Goodwill. I wore those for at least the first year and changed blouses. I still looked professional and put together.

You don't need to spend tons of money on clothes, but dress as if you are in a position of authority, because you are. You are not only representing yourself, but your clients. In alignment with maintaining femininity, select appropriate accessories. Wear some jewelry, but avoid bulky, flashy jewelry that can be distracting. Select simple pieces that can be paired with different outfits. You should want to put your best foot forward when representing yourself. Wear some makeup, find a hairstyle that compliments you, do what you can to look professional and polished at all times.

Appearance is more than just clothes. Take pride in your overall appearance and hygiene because it can affect your reputation and other people's opinion of you. I remember a female attorney who only owned a handful of suits. After a year or so, she started wearing the same black jacket and pants every day, just with a different blouse. Well, we were both working at the same firm and one of the partners approached me and said, "Could you speak to her about her clothing?" and I said that I would. He asked me to talk to her because I dressed in the manner that was in line with how the partners dressed. They always looked polished from head to toe, and so did I, so he tasked me with this request.

I talked to her and she didn't want to hear it. She brushed it off, and when I asked her why she wore the same thing all the time, she attributed it to her family background. Eventually, the office manager, who was not an attorney and was also a man, had to talk to her and inform her that her coworkers were complaining about her hygiene. Naturally, she was upset at being confronted, and I am sure it was very embarrassing for her. Those are not conversations that anybody wants to have with anyone, but if you're out there and you're doing your business every day, you should be clean, and you should look well-kept. It doesn't matter what kind of job you have—you're not going to be thought of as somebody that cares about herself.

The truth is, first impressions are everything. As uncomfortable as it may be, we are constantly under the microscope. Judged by colleagues, employees, and others, how we look and dress influences treatment and perception. Personal hygiene and grooming, can either help or hinder assumptions of competency.

Another note – never, NEVER wear too much perfume. It can be overpowering and off-putting. Although they may seem superficial or frivolous, all of these things are important. Put effort into how you look, dress, and appear to others. Ask your friends and family to give you feedback. Don't get offended if they say something you don't like. Most importantly, listen to them and be open-minded to their advice.

Chapter 5.

Carrying Yourself

After I got my first job working for the District Attorney, I met a lot of attorneys. During that period of time, he had a couple of female attorneys working for him. I am forever grateful to those women because they had a lot in common. They were not overly aggressive, but they also didn't back down. When you're a prosecutor, you hardly ever have to back down. I learned that demeanor from them. They were all very classy, confident people who knew how to handle themselves.

I see too many female attorneys who don't make their presence truly known. It even shows in their body language, almost as if they're trying to hide. They walk with their heads down, they don't smile very often, and they seem to do everything to keep attention off themselves.

I never had this problem, because I am a very confident person and I carry myself that way. I always make sure my hair looks good and that my make-up is done. Even if I'm just wearing jeans, I make sure they are good jeans–not to work, or course. I like to walk with my head up, I like to smile at people, engage with them. When I talk with people I look them straight in the eye, in a friendly, warm way, never coming across as aggressive. No matter who I meet, I am always polite and always extend a hand.

Acknowledge those you come across, greet people, introduce yourself. It's amazing how many people don't even say hello to each other anymore, especially in New England. There are many people that don't say hello back to me, but I don't care. You have to understand that this is a people business, and carrying yourself in a good way conveys that to people.

For example, I practice etiquette. As an attorney, there are fine lines between appropriate and inappropriate behavior. I have seen a lot of attorneys make stupid little mistakes in their interactions with other lawyers, judges, and clients. Be polite to people. Don't try to push people around. Just because you're a lawyer doesn't mean you have the power to intimidate other people. Even if you are arguing with another lawyer or trying to make a point, always remain polite.

I always try to keep my cool because as soon as somebody starts getting hot-headed, the discussion is going to start to go down the tubes. Whatever you are doing, if you are negotiating with someone that's adverse to you, just be polite and try to be engaging. Don't treat them like an adversary, treat them like you are solving this problem together, and if that person pushes you off, that's their problem, not yours.

Whatever you are doing, be respectful and aware of what's going on around you, especially when it comes to other people's time. Be prepared in court. Don't stand there staring at your phone while the judge is waiting for you to set the next court date–you should already know in advance and have 2-3 dates of when you can come back.

The same applies to clients: remember meetings, and be places on time. Don't waste time. Yours or theirs. You've got to know your next move. Think two-steps ahead–what's the end result of this conversation? What's the result of this court date supposed to be? You should be able to look down the road and know what you are going to do.

Bottom line is that you always have to be aware that whoever you are talking to in this business is judging you. All the time. One of the things that people judge lawyers on the most is how knowledgeable we come across and how knowledgeable we are of other people. If you can't show a client, another lawyer, or a judge that you understand people, and what this person needs or wants from you, they are not going to want to work with you.

You've also got to judge yourself while you are in your practice. When interacting with other people, be aware of what you are saying. Ask yourself if you said something that may have been taken the wrong way or misconstrued. I'm very sensitive when it comes to conversations and how I interact with people, but sometimes somebody's just having a bad day and they snap at you.

You might say something that you would always say in polite conversation and they reacted negatively. You know it's not your fault, so you move on, but it's important to be aware of how you come across. Notice if you're snapping at people or being confrontational.

There are lawyers that I know who have a very brash manner about them. No one can stand them. One female attorney in particular is very off-putting. She is unkind and uses her words to push people around. The way she comes across has created a negative perception, and nobody wants to be around her. Make sure that you are not the lawyer that people go around talking about.

Because if you are, it means that you are not successfully navigating this business. You are not doing something right, and you either need to figure it out and address it, or you are never going to be a partner or have your own successful law firm. A standoffish attitude will not get you very far, and people will not want to work with you.

Remember that you are not better than anybody else. Don't be prideful or use your words to put other people down. When interacting with other people, keep your tone neutral and focus on fostering positive relationships with those around you. Treat everyone with respect and use your voice for good. Another aspect to consider is body language. Be aware of your physical movements and mannerisms.

If you are a nail biter, quit. If you have any nervous habits, stop doing them. I knew somebody who always used to put her hand over her mouth when she was talking. I know she did it when she was nervous, but it drove me crazy. She was really smart and articulate, but she had this bad habit that distracted from her abilities.

I remember when I met up with her fifteen years later and she was still doing it. I said to her, "I can't believe you still cover your mouth all the time." She replied that people were always telling her about it and I just wondered why she hadn't done anything about it. She's in Law School now and she really wants to go to court, but I told her that if she goes to court and puts her hand over her mouth when she's talking to a judge, they are going to hand your ass to you and embarrass you in front of a room full of people. They won't even think twice about it. That's not something that you ever want to have happen in front of a client or colleagues.

I knew another female attorney who also had a nervous habit. Every time she was giving a statement to the court, she would pull her long sleeves down over her hands. I could never figure out why she did this, but it was very distracting. Another lawyer I know speaks so fast that you can't keep up with what she is saying. If she talked to a judge like that, she would be asked to slow down.

It's a bad habit among a lot of people, but it really needs to be worked on. You've got to be able to know how you sound to people. If you are talking too fast, people will tell you. Be conscious of the speed at which you speak. You want to come across as a solid, good talker. Somebody who means what they say and says what they mean.

When considering body language, try to keep an open stance, especially when addressing a judge. Avoid folding the arms, as it comes across as aggressive. It sends out bad body language signals and people will not react well to that. An aggressive stance also expresses a sense of arrogance. I know a few attorneys who are arrogant, and it's off-putting. Keep your attitude in check. No successful attorneys or judges will tolerate it.

These are examples of things that can all be fixed. What it comes down to is confidence. Be sure about yourself. Many women lack confidence in certain professional fields, and law is one of them. Don't let yourself be intimidated. You are a lawyer who just happens to be a woman. Don't think of yourself as female or male. Just think lawyering–that's all.

If a judge asks you what appears to be a sexist question, don't be defensive, just smile and rise above it. I've had judges say things to me that were a little out of line, and I called them on it, but I didn't go overboard about it. I knew this one judge, an Italian guy, who was known for not liking female attorneys, but he always liked me. He also liked my firm, which was good because a lot of the other judges didn't. I think he liked me because I'm friendly, smart, I smile a lot, and I take care in my appearance.

One day he called me into his office and said he wanted to hold the meeting there. It was me, him, the court reporter, and another attorney. I was sitting next to the wall and when we were all finished with what we needed to talk about the judge says to me, "Turn to your right and look at that picture." So, I do, and I find myself looking at a photograph of the Yale graduating class from about 1940, or something like that. "Oh, did you go to Yale?" I asked. And he says, "Yes, I did and I am very proud of that because they didn't let Italians in back then. "

So, he then asks me if I can find the famous person in the photo and I immediately spotted President George Bush! He remarked at how fast I had noticed that and seemed impressed by it. After this interaction, I think he decided he liked me, which was really kind of cool.

Here I was, in front of a judge that's known for not liking women, but I had managed to win him over. I couldn't change his perception, but I got him to like me. I also did with another judge. He was known for being rough around the edges, like Archie Bunker, from the bench. He didn't swear or anything like that, but you could tell that he was not born with a silver spoon in his mouth and that he got to where he was through hard work and determination. One day he chewed me out bad. I didn't back down and I stayed firm, but I knew that this treatment would not have happened to a male attorney.

There are a lot of situations that I've been in which would have been different outcomes if I had been a man. One time I was at court and I needed an interpreter for one of my clients. His daughter informed me of the language and I made that request to the Clerk's Office, which is what you're supposed to do. I made my request and left. The day before I was due in court, around four o'clock in the afternoon, I got a call from the Clerk's Office.

The woman on the line introduced herself and said, "We don't have an interpreter for you tomorrow." I replied that it was okay and she proceeded to tell me that they had tried but there was nobody available, however, she wanted to put the case on for a later date. I told her, "I can't really do that because the defendant has already driven from New York to Boston today and he's staying in Boston with his daughter. They were coming in tomorrow and I didn't want to tell him he's got to drive back to New York. So, it's not really necessary. "

I was trying to explain to her that based on what he was charged with, in my experience with the prosecutors there, I had a pretty good idea of what was going to happen and was sure we didn't need to be in front of a judge. As I'm explaining this, she just wouldn't listen to me. She starts raising her voice, taking my explanation as a personal attack on her and her office. I calmly say, "I'm not accusing you of anything. I'm trying to tell you that it's no big deal and that it's okay. I'm going to still have the Court."

At this point, she's absolutely irate. I'm not sure why she's so upset, this whole time I'm still just trying to be polite, but she would not listen to me and kept talking over me. I eventually finish what I am saying and hang up the phone.

I go in there the next day, and I come across a woman who works in the District Attorney's Office. She can be funny at times, but she has an edge that also makes her hard to like. As I walk in the door she says to me, "So, I heard that you fought with somebody in the Clerk's Office yesterday." I said, "What? What are you talking about?" She tells me that the woman I was on the phone with had told her that I was really mean to her. I explained that I hadn't been mean to her and tried to give her some understanding of the conversation.

She then tells me that I should apologize and make things right. I agreed to apologize even though I knew I had done nothing wrong, but you know what, I've got to come here for the next fifteen years, so I'll apologize.

I went to her and said, "Sorry if I came across that way, I really didn't mean to." And as I'm apologizing to her, she starts to talk over me again. I let it go because it was her problem and not mine. She did not do her job like she was supposed to and wouldn't admit it, but I didn't want to make a big deal out of it. After this incident I remember thinking to myself, "You know what, I know they wouldn't do this to me if I was a male attorney."

Truth is, if I had been a man, I would never have been told to apologize to her, but I didn't care. You can't let people rattle you, especially when they're the ones we need to help solve the problem. Look past it, rise above it, apologize if necessary, or at least acknowledge that you meant no harm to them.

I am always polite to people, even when it doesn't always work in my favor. I want to be aware of how I come across. I was polite to this woman even when she started a fight with me. Even now when I go back to that court, I still act as if nothing has ever happened. Female attorneys are often cast with a "bitch" stereotype that we have to play down, but the truth is, I love people. I want to be around them and help them. I love helping people, and I don't care if my client is male or female, or what race they are, if they need my help, I'm there. Arguing with people gets you nowhere in this business. Always be polite and professional, even if a client, judge, or another lawyer is behaving inappropriately.

When it comes to differences between female and male attorneys, one thing that I have noticed is that men don't overanalyze everything, and neither should women. Lawyers are naturally analytical people. I have been like that my whole life. If something is nagging at me, I have gotten on the phone with an attorney or a friend and try to get their feedback. I focus on what they're saying to me because they usually tell me that I'm worrying too much.

You really must avoid that, because analysis leads to paralysis. Somebody said that to me once and it stuck with me. If you overanalyze, you are unable to think on your feet and let things go. You've got to know when to hold on to things and when to let things go.

Once you free yourself from overthinking about things, you can move forward without hesitation. Get rid of doubts – all of them. This is a very difficult business. Being a lawyer is not easy. It's competitive, and there are going to be people who won't like you, and for no real reason. Don't internalize those feelings. Stick it out. Go workout, have dinner with your friends, watch a movie. Do something to take your mind off of what you do for a living when you find it's bringing you down so that you have an escape.

If you're doubting yourself, it's going to come across to people, and it will not make you look good as a lawyer. Doubt in your own time, in the privacy of your home. Think to yourself about what you could have done differently and how to improve for the next time. Clients want you to be confident and knowledgeable. Nobody wants a lawyer who's unsure of herself.

Chapter 6.

Using Your Voice

I remember that when Katie Couric was on the Today Show in the mornings, she was upbeat. A lot of morning shows try to keep it lighthearted and feature fun stories and that sort of thing. I remember thinking that she was very good at sounding happy when she needed to be, but could also change her tone and sound sad when she had to.

If it was a positive story, she was upbeat and fun, but if they were covering a tragedy that had happened, her voice would change immediately. She could go from focusing on who had won the heavyweight championship fight to talking about a bus load of school kids that ran off the road. I remember I always liked watching her because I just thought, wow, she is good at using her voice.

As much as law is a people business, it's also a communication business. This is what we do. We are supposed to be the masters of words, and a lawyer who doesn't have the right words is not going to have a practice for very long. If you don't know how to speak to people, and I mean all people, you will not be successful.

Just remember to think before you speak. There is a right and wrong way to speak to a judge, a client, and opposing counsel. All interactions require different volume levels and tones. You've got to get those things down. If you are aware of how you sound, you have more control. Just remember to make sure that you are not coming across as pushy or arrogant. When you go to court, be confident. Use clear, concise language and eliminate informal language like "ums" and "huhs". You have to understand who you are talking to and what they want from you.

More importantly, we need to also know how to listen to that person. Your voice is a tool. As a professional, you should sound like it. I have come across many female attorneys who are very soft-spoken. When they talk, they often raise their voice at the end of a statement. This inflection sounds as if they are asking a question, even when they aren't.

Women tend to want to please people instead of making statements that are definitive and certain. If you make statements and use an upward inflection, you sound like you are unsure of yourself, and people pick up on this. It's a lot like acting—act the part, and when you're speaking to another person, make sure what you're saying is appropriate for the conversation.

If you are soft-spoken, work with a voice coach. After a few sessions, you'll be able to learn with the help of someone who understands voice and how it works. Very quickly, they will be able to tell you what you need to do in order to improve your speech.

When I am speaking to an older individual, for example, somebody in their eighties, I'm very polite, I call them Mr. And Mrs. , and to show respect, I never call them by their first name. I speak a little slower just to make sure that they are getting everything I'm saying, and I study their face as I'm talking to them.

A lot of people are too intimidated by lawyers to say, "I don't understand what you just said." So you have to watch them as you're speaking to them. If they looked puzzled or if you notice any kind of a look that seems uncertain, you stop and ask them if you are making sense.

Don't say something along the lines of, "Do you understand me?" Because that's condescending. I put it on me, I want to be explaining things in a way that's easy for people to understand. Don't try to use big words or difficult language, because people don't like being spoken to that way. Nobody likes being talked down to, so avoid doing that. I'll say something like, "If I'm not making sense, please tell me, and I'll find another way to say it."

As a lawyer, no matter who you're talking to, you should never talk down to anybody. I have heard lawyers do it and I think it's a disgusting trait. Again, you are NOT better than anybody else. Remember, whoever you are talking to is expecting something. Live up to that expectation, and exceed it if you can.

For example, if you're talking to somebody who has been badly injured, you have to show compassion to that person. Even if you can't understand exactly how they're feeling, at least show some empathy so that they can feel like you understand where they are coming from.

Chances are, you've never been severely injured, but there are those who are in a wheelchair and can't move. Or maybe they broke their arm after slipping on some ice in front of a building and it wasn't their fault. Whatever it is, choose your words carefully and make sure that you're being understood.

There was a lawyer that used to work at the same firm as I did, and she would always have her door shut. I never shut my door, because it was not that kind of firm. None of the partners or other attorneys ever had their doors shut, but she always did. One day I went up to her and said, "Why do you always have your door shut?" She was very honest with me and explained, "Because I think I sound stupid and I don't want any of the people at the firm to overhear me." This was happening early on, when she had just started working there, and I explained to her that she was missing out on a learning opportunity.

I expounded on that by explaining to her that those paralegals on the other side of the door know more than she does, and with her door shut, she would never get to hear them talk. I told her, "If you kept your door open, you would be able to hear them speak, and you would learn this language a lot faster, because every area of law has its own language and you have to learn it. "

When you don't know what something is and you don't ask questions, you will not succeed as a lawyer. Using your voice means being confident enough in your abilities to ask about what things mean. If you don't want to ask someone, look it up, take out your law dictionary. I have my law dictionary with me and I use it all the time.

Don't be intimidated by people who know more than you do; in fact, use it to your advantage. Get a second opinion, run things by other lawyers, I do it all the time. I've been practicing for 25 years and I still call other attorneys daily to say, "What do you think of this? What do you think this judge is going to do?" Or, if they are familiar with the judge, I may ask advice about how to approach my case. Learn from your colleagues. Lawyers love to talk to other lawyers, it's a way of bonding and a reminder that you're not in this alone.

A long time ago, one of my friends told me about a certain situation where she had walked out of the courtroom and another lawyer followed her out. As she was walking out he stopped her and asked, "What's the matter?" She was just really flustered and told him that she didn't really know how to handle the situation because she was not familiar with the attorney.

He managed to find out what her problem was, and he helped her navigate the situation. Afterwards he said to her, "Look, you should feel like you can call any lawyer in the Connecticut Bar, get them on the phone, and talk to them about this. Learn from other attorneys."

I always remembered that. This took place years ago but I always remembered it because that is what I decided to do. You can save so much time when you talk to other attorneys that know more than you do. They can tell you about the eccentricities of a firm, judge, or lawyer. Some lawyers get very well known, especially the older you are. There are attorneys in Connecticut that are in their sixties and seventies and they still love taking phone calls from people they barely know. They'll get on the phone and talk to you for a few minutes. Call them. They are a wealth of knowledge. If you are kind and polite to other attorneys, they are going to want to help you.

Take that chance. Call people on the phone, introduce yourself, and ask them if they'll help you with something. If the person says no, call somebody else. We women often question ourselves more than men do and as a lawyer, it can either help you or hinder you. Use your voice to improve your career.

Chapter 7.

Managing Your Emotions

Every day that I'm in court, I see emotion. All of the time. I always see people walking out of court crying, both men and women. People are trying not to be emotional, and sometimes they aren't because they're not really facing anything very serious, but many people can't help it. Law is emotional because it regulates human behavior and naturally, humans are emotional. As a lawyer, you have to feel what you're doing, your heart has to be in it. Have a heart and don't be afraid to show it, but you have to be able to manage your emotions.

I was in court one day and a friend of mine, who had a very big case going on in Massachusetts, couldn't be there, so I said that I would go and listen to the appeal. While I was there, a lot of the appeals that were getting brought into the upper courts were criminal appeals. His wasn't, but I was sitting there watching the public defenders. I noticed one woman who was representing a client who was in a lot of trouble and as she's giving her presentation, she stops, mid-sentence.

Understand, when you do the appellate court, it's not like a trial. Nobody can jump in or object, the only thing that can throw you off kilter is the judges asking you questions. Appellate court is big time. It means somebody's life is on the line, their freedom, or their livelihood. Something is on the line and they stand to lose a lot.

So, I'm watching this public defender present and she's talking, she's doing okay. She's fine and then all of the sudden, she's not talking any more. She was presenting to two men and a woman, and the female judge picked up on this. There was silence for about ten or fifteen seconds and the female judge says to her, "Do you need a few minutes? Do you need a break?" The defense lawyer, who at this point was visibly upset, answered that she did, so they called a recess. This lawyer was crying, and she didn't stop, even as she rushed out of the courtroom.

I remember her being young and thinking that if I was her boss right now, I would probably be upset. You have a very important case and as a public defender, you're probably going to get fired. As I said, you are in the appellate court, this is serious, and you really need to be better prepared. Of course, I didn't say anything to her in person, but I had thought of going and giving her a pep-talk, and decided against it. Truth is, I didn't know her and figured she would learn from this, come back next time and finish, and that's exactly what she did.

This is a prime example of the importance of handling your emotions during difficult situations. She ended up being alright in the end, but this scenario could have gone a lot differently if she had different judges on that day. Let's say she didn't have nice judges, they would have just said, "What's your problem? This is the appellate court, wipe your tears and keep going." You DO have to have a heart when you practice, but you also have to understand that it's not your life. You're helping someone else, and their stories are going to be emotional.

One day I sat in court listening to a mom reading a letter about her daughter who had died. As she's reading, I was tearing up and had to keep wiping my eyes because listening to the letter was heartbreaking. Absolutely heartbreaking. That's expected. You will get emotional from time to time, but you probably shouldn't display that when you are the one making the presentation to the court.

Sometimes tapping into an emotionally charged case can be effective, other times, it's not. I watched a female public defender make her closing statement in a Massachusetts court. She was crying as the delivered her final words, and I remember thinking how strange it was. She ended up winning the case, but I don't think it was because she was emotional throughout it, in fact, I don't think anybody in that courtroom thought it was effective. The jury may have, but they also could have just chosen to not hold it against her. Emotion aside, I think the real reason she won the case was because it was a strong case – the woman she was representing had been battered, and that helped her get a not guilty verdict.

All in all, you must be very prepared for emotional cases and it's okay to show your feelings once in a while. That doesn't mean you sit there and break down in the middle of the courtroom because you're representing somebody, and you've got to do a good job for them. I mean, I got choked up when one of my clients was getting sentenced.

He was a young guy who had screwed up and he knew he was going to be doing some time, and standing there listening to the judge was really hard. I could feel myself getting emotional, like I was about to start crying. I knew I couldn't interrupt the judge, so I just had to focus on something else for about ten seconds until that feeling went away.

I think that if you aren't going to have any emotion in your law practice, why are you doing it? Somebody's calling you because they have a problem and you need to represent them. And oftentimes, it's going to be an emotional case. Ignoring that doesn't make it go away. Accept that there are going to be times when you get emotional. Don't shut down your emotion just because it's difficult.

You have to get to the point where you have enough confidence in yourself that, even if you do get a little emotional about something, you own it. Simply say, "I'm sorry. I didn't mean to be emotional about this, but this is a really hard case for me." If you acknowledge it, people will probably understand.

Men seem to have it easier than women in some ways. I'm not a man, but they seem to be able to just shut it off, like a faucet. Women are usually not like that, and I never worry about being emotional because if it ever happens, I will acknowledge it and move on. If you are in touch with your emotions, you will be a better lawyer.

One of my clients recently thanked me for being so supportive. He's 20-years old and was in a lot of trouble. He never meant to get into trouble, but he was hanging around the wrong people and ended up being in this situation. As awful as the situation was, he texted me and said, "I really can't thank you enough for being so supportive."

As a female attorney, I think it's easier to show that I really care about you, whereas if a man does it, it might be misconstrued, especially if it's towards a female client. In a lot of ways, I think that having emotions about things benefits a female attorney. When my clients are upset, I am always very understanding and open my heart to that person.

I tell them that I really care about what happens to them and that yes, I am being paid to represent you, but I care about what's happening. If they need me, all they need to do is call me. To talk about the case or even if they are feeling down and need a pep-talk. Whatever it is, I want to reassure them that everything is going to work out. I put myself in my client's shoes and let them know that I'm there for them and they really appreciate it.

I think a lot of female attorneys try to distance themselves from the way that they feel about something and that's just something I never do. I try not to just practice with my head, but also from my heart. I put my heart into everything I do. Men obviously get emotional about things as well, but as women, we have a natural advantage because we perceive things more emotionally than men do. Clients respond positively when they know they are cared about.

If a lawyer just comes across as dry and cerebral, that can be off-putting to people. With that approach, you can find yourself getting away from how you feel about things. Don't shut it off. I think it's important for attorneys, especially for women attorneys, not to shut that off. Just accept that it's a part of who you are, and that letting yourself feel things will help your practice.

Chapter 8.

Listening on Purpose

In this job, you will have to tell people things that they don't want to hear. On the other hand, you will also hear about very difficult things as well. Don't be afraid to hear those things. People need to feel that they can say what needs to be said. They should be able to talk to their lawyer, no matter how unsettling or personal the conversation is. Listening is such an important skill to have because it allows you to connect with people.

When a conversation is taking place between myself and client, I want them to be able to talk freely without interruption. Whether in person or on the phone, I let them talk without saying anything or making remarks. The occasional affirmative "mm-hm" is usually appropriate, just so they know that I'm still there on the other end of the phone.

Because I'm so intently listening, sometimes the clients will ask, "Are you there?" Almost as if they are surprised that a lawyer is actually listening to them. I think it's a skill that many lawyers need to work on. Sometimes it's just important to shut up and listen, just let them talk to you. Listen to understand, not just to respond.

When meeting with a client, it's a consultation. Yes, you are evaluating what they are saying, but you are also just having a conversation, that's the goal. You're not sitting there analyzing them or second guessing them. You want to listen and make them feel comfortable instead of trying to figure out things. You may not master this right off the bat, but over time, you should be able to figure out the best way that works for you.

Sometimes lawyers wait for clients to say certain things so that they can show how smart they are and respond appropriately. You don't need to do that very often because when someone needs to be heard, they need to be heard. They don't necessarily need you to show them how much you know as a lawyer in that moment.

When you are face to face with clients, don't take notes, unless absolutely necessary. It's a habit we all developed in law school, but you have to outgrow it. The reason why it's important not to take notes is because it's rude to the client if you're sitting with them and you start writing down everything they're saying. If you're a paralegal, or a brand new lawyer, you can tell that person, "I need to write down what you're saying. I'm listening to you intently, but I need to write it down so that I remember everything." As a seasoned attorney however, you won't need to do that.

I remember it was my old boss who got me out of that habit. Whenever I would go and sit at his desk, as he would be explaining something to me, I would write everything down. He let me do that for about a year and then after that he said, "Do not come into my office with a pen and paper. You're going to listen to me and that's all you're going to do."

It was really good to have somebody like that, forcing me stop taking notes, because that is such a lawyer thing, we all do it. There are times when it's appropriate to write down everything that's being said, like during a trial, but it's not appropriate when you're talking to someone.

One of the things about most attorneys, myself included, is that we like to talk. As important as it is to be a good speaker, it is also important to be a good listener and sometimes, you have to be both.

There are times when I've had clients that I had to pull information out of. They want to get the case over with, but they usually leave out important information. In order to get what I need from them, I have found that active listening also has to do with asking a lot of questions. When I'm talking to a client, I can usually tell within the first thirty seconds whether or not they understand what information is going to be the most useful for me.

To make sure I don't get a whole bunch of information that I don't need, I guide the conversation by asking questions. Most people are relieved, because they're usually not sure about what information is really the most relevant to their case. Even if I ask most of the questions, I always try to be polite in the first minutes of the conversation, making sure not to cut them off because that's rude. I never want my clients to feel rushed, because I truly want to help them. If they're talking and start going off track, I bring them back to where they should be and keep going.

My conversation style is appreciated by a lot of people because I treat my clients like they're really important, because they are. I try my best to be a good listener, but there are times when I've found myself talking to a client and not liking what they were saying. Still, I have to remind myself to listen anyway, which can be difficult to do, especially when the client doesn't know what they're talking about. It's a frustrating experience for me because sometimes, clients can take advantage of that.

There have been times when I've been on the phone with somebody who I wouldn't let hire me because they came across as being too verbally aggressive. I don't mind listening to somebody, but when people start out conversations acting as if I somehow caused their problem, I will not let them hire me, and if I have the chance, I will tell them why.

In cases like this, I'll just keep telling them over and over, "I'm not the right lawyer for you." Sometimes they get indignant and go, "Well, why not?" As much as I'm dying to say, "Because you won't listen to a word I have to say, so I don't know how I can possibly represent you." I settle for, "I'm just not the right lawyer for you" and leave it at that.

Just recently I had a guy call me and he started a conversation out by blaming the cops, prosecutor, and judge. Blaming everyone is never a good start with me. Yes, it could be a possibility, everyone makes mistakes, but judges and prosecutors have to follow the book. I usually look up their case and see that they have another similar case, proving to me that I'm probably not the right lawyer for them, especially if they're not willing to admit they've had this problem before.

In this instance, I didn't let this man hire me because I knew that he was in the wrong. Sure, we're in a difficult court, but I knew that he was the problem, not the cops, not the prosecutor, and certainly not me. I am not one of those lawyers that can stand getting bullied by anybody, and I won't. I know other attorneys who put up with it and I never understand why. Listening on purpose not only has to do with hearing what the other person is saying, but it also means figuring out if you're the right person to represent them. If you don't think that you are, and they don't think you are, then you've got your answer.

In this case, I didn't want him as a client, but I also remained polite and diplomatic about how I handled the situation. Instead of sending them off empty handed, I'll sometimes guide them in the right direction and give them a referral of a lawyer I know that would work better for them. In other situations, I'll just say, "I'm sorry, I really don't know who you should call" because I really don't know who they should call. I make decisions based on the situation, but I always do what I think is best. Not only is listening needed for effective communication, but it's also necessary when making business decisions and whether or not you'll accept clients based on what they tell you.

Chapter 9.

Building Your Reputation

All you have is integrity. If you get known as somebody that's not to be trusted, that is going to follow you around. Depending on the lawyers you associate with, that will either happen quickly or over a period of time. Eventually, you will get a reputation and you will not be able to change it. I remember a lawyer who ended up leaving her job, which is strange because most people in her position don't leave their government jobs.

No one could really find out why she chose to leave. She seemed to like her job and she wasn't fired, but the only thing I could think of was her reputation. I knew a lot of lawyers who did not trust her. She did not treat people very well, and many people couldn't stand to work with her.

As a female attorney, you have to be careful not to get known as being brash or a push-over, and make sure that you are known as a nice person. The work we do, no matter what kind of work, can be very difficult, so you've really got to figure out how to deal with that difficulty while also maintaining a professional attitude towards everyone, towards opposing counsel, towards your client, and towards anybody else that you're dealing with. Whatever it is you're doing, make sure that you are aware of how people view you.

As a female attorney, it's also important that you are not getting known as somebody who sleeps around. In this one area of life, if you are known for anything at all, sex is going ruin your career and it's usually a scandal that's hard to come up from.

I once represented a client who was known for going out with a girl who had been known to sleep around. Turns out, she ended up getting dismissed from the Army National Guard and so did the people she had been associated with, as well as my client. I'm not kidding when I say that careers have been ruined by sex because they have. This plays out in all professions, but it is particularly damaging for lawyers.

So, how do you know if you have a good reputation or not? Ask your clients. The best way to think of yourself is not by thinking you're a good lawyer but by listing your traits. Are you honest? Thorough? At this point in my life, I don't even know what someone means when they say this person's a good lawyer. Usually when they're describing these attorneys they're saying how smart they are. That they're easy to talk to. They're the type of attorney who would stop what they are doing to help another attorney, this kind of thing. These are all great things but, on some days, you have to shine brighter than the others.

This is a very competitive field and only the strong survive. The strong are honest, hardworking people who don't go where they shouldn't be. I once knew a guy, a very nice person, probably in his early thirties, who was always smiling and saying hi to everybody. He got elected to public office in the city he was raised in so that was really great, because he eventually became even more well known.

Unfortunately, he wasn't paying attention and got involved with a group of people he had no business getting involved with. He didn't have his lawyer gauge up and all he saw was the money. Before he knew it, he was assisting them in committing crimes. He was young and he got too far into it. He wanted the hot car and the expensive suits, and he just didn't think about the consequences. Well, it caught up to him and now he's sitting in federal prison. He got disbarred and is serving time. It's sad because he really is a great guy, but he made decisions that cost him his career.

As a lawyer, you have to trust your gut in order to protect your reputation, because if somebody's asking you to do something that seems strange, run. This guy didn't figure it out right off the bat. The best thing he could have done was get away from these people, but he ended up doing the smart thing. When people found out, he had enough information to provide to the federal authorities. Because of this, I think they went a bit lighter on him, but he's never going to be able to practice law again. Talk about going out of your law career in one of the worst ways ever.

The lesson here is that if it sounds too good to be true, it probably is. As a lawyer, to build a good reputation, you have to have good instincts. A guy I know, who's in his early 70s, is still actively practicing law. Just recently he told me he turned away a five-million-dollar deal. He's a real estate attorney, he was probably going to make about $50,000 off of that deal, but something wasn't right. He couldn't put his finger on exactly what it was, but he just kept telling me that there was something wrong with this deal. He ended up declining the offer because he felt unsure about it, and probably dodged a bullet in the process.

That's the thing, you have always got to have your guard up. It's not that you never trust anybody, you've just got to pay attention. If someone tells you something that just doesn't sound right, or there's something about it that you don't like, just politely tell that person, "I'm not the right lawyer for you." Know this: if you do choose to get in with people that you shouldn't, it will come back to bite you. You will end up losing your license and you could possibly end up going to jail.

This guy wasn't the first lawyer I know who went to jail, I know another attorney who ended up in jail. He was also young and getting a lot of real estate deals from a man who had tried to hire me a few times. I had always said no. One of my best friends kept getting mad at me because I wouldn't do this guy's deals. I had to say to her, "Look, I don't trust this guy. There's something wrong, something slippery about him. I can't put my finger on it, and I'm sorry that you're mad at me, but I'm not doing his deals."

She ended up eating her words when another lawyer who did his deals ended up losing his license and going to jail. The guy was a snake, and even when the lawyer figured it out, he didn't step away because the money was too good. He probably didn't think he was going to get caught because attorneys make that mistake. They don't think it's going to happen to them. In their minds, who's going to know? Who's going to find out? In the end, they get found out and there's no one else there to take the fall.

A lawyer I know will always say, "Does it pass the smell test? If it doesn't then you have to push it away." I remember learning that no deal, no one case or transaction is worth losing your license over. Unfortunately, some attorneys don't grasp that. Could you get away with it? Maybe, but you shouldn't even try.

Another way to build your reputation is to talk to other lawyers. If somebody is asking you to do something, and you're not

100% sure about it, call up some of your lawyer friends. Tell them about what you were asked to do and they'll explain whether it's illegal or not. If you don't listen to the advice of other attorneys, you're never going to be a good lawyer, and you could end up in a world of trouble.

This is the type of field that can be all consuming. You have to try to step away from it sometimes. Whatever you do, you always have to think about helping people before you think about money. Make sure that everyone who knows you knows that you are an honest person that they can trust. They should know that when you say something, you're telling the truth.

If you're an honest person, you should be able to tell if other people are being honest with you. When a client tells me something, sometimes I will say, "Okay, now tell me what really happened" because I know that they're lying to me but I don't want to directly ask them that. I'll usually just explain that I heard what they had said but that there were some things that weren't making sense to me. Usually people will come clean and say, "You know what, fine. You're right. I wasn't being truthful, here's what really happened." Once they tell me the true story, it all makes sense. Getting to the truth will make you a better lawyer and secure your credibility.

To maintain a good reputation, occasionally, do something nice for someone, at no cost. A couple times a year I do pro bono work. Let's say, a young kid calls me, petrified of telling their parents. They don't have any money, but I tell them what to do to help them get out of trouble. Another example is providing information.

If somebody is calling me and I'm not the person they need, because they need a divorce attorney or something like that, I'll give them a little bit of information to guide them in the right direction. I'll give them a few names of the people in the area and provide them with somewhere to start. You always want to be known as someone who's approachable and who people can call on. If people know that you're going to be upfront and honest with them, that is the best reputation to have.

As you build you practice, your reputation also hinges on your professional behavior. Be prepared. When you go to court and you're not prepared, people will notice that. I always make sure that I'm prepared for court or other appointments. If I'm going to meet with other attorneys to talk about something, I read up on something before I go if it's something that I'm not familiar with. I was working on a Supreme Court appeal and thankfully, one of the guys on the team there had a lot of experience doing appeals. I defer to him all the time. I don't pretend to know all the answers, I'll always admit if I don't know something.

One of my professors in law school said that when he was a practicing lawyer, he never liked it. He was honest with us and told us that he didn't like being a lawyer, but he loved the law. He was a really smart guy, and I remember him telling us, preparation can be done in place of years of experience.

One of the things he said was that he had won cases going up against lawyers that were a lot more experienced than he was. These were lawyers who had been doing this for a long time. As a newbie, he was so panicked about losing and doing a good job for his client that he just lived it. Breathed it. Slept it. All to make sure that when he walked into that courtroom, he was beyond prepared.

If you have that reputation, when you stand up in front of a judge, they will know who you are. They know that you'll have something valuable to say. Even if they don't know you, you should still have something valuable to say. The only way to do that is to be overly prepared or at the very least, thoroughly prepared. Once you get going with whatever it is you're doing, the preparation will show. Whether you crammed it, like you do for a final exam, or whether you've been doing it for five years, if you're doing your best, it will show.

Chapter 10.

Creating Trust

As a lawyer, not only do you want to create trust with your clients, but you always want to be sure that trust extends to other individuals in the field, namely, other attorneys and judges. Truth is, having people trust you and knowing that you are trustworthy can make or break your practice. This doesn't mean you can't make a mistake, it just means that you are honest in your business and you are honest with those around you.

People trust me because I don't lie or stretch the truth. I also make sure that I don't talk about people behind their backs or get into petty arguments. If my clients have full trust in me, I am not going to betray that. There are some times when I need to tell a judge something about a client, that is usually embarrassing or extremely personal. I have no problem telling things to a judge that my client would not want me to say in open court, but I think the judge needs to know this about my client, so I say it in chambers, off the record.

Judges, at least in Connecticut, are very tactful about it and they won't say anything on the record that they think is going to make anybody upset. I don't use it to exploit anybody, and I never say anything unless I think it's important to the case.

No one has to trust you. Trust has to be earned. It has to do with caring about people. When people call you and need you, they should know that they can trust you and that you're not going to take advantage of them. Years ago, probate attorneys could just charge people whatever they wanted. The reason why this is a problem is because you're finding out all about this person's assets. Now you know how much money they have in the bank when they die or how many children are going to be inheriting that money.

A long time ago, I remember a woman whose husband had just died. She told me that she had used a lawyer, who I happened to know, but did not like. He didn't have many friends and was a little obnoxious. As she's telling me about him, she told me that he had charged her around $20,000 to settle her husband's estate. So, she asked him how he knew it was going to be $20,000, because nobody was inheriting anything yet. She owned the house and wasn't going to sell it outright, and she also didn't have anything to sell.

He said, "Well, it's just a retainer. It's enough for a retainer because I don't know how much I'm going to actually have to use." She agreed and writes him this check for $20,000.

She was an educated person, but she was really nice and didn't want to ruffle feathers, so she didn't ask any further questions. After everything was said and done, he sends her a bill for $20,000. One of her sons calls him and says, "Where'd you come up with this figure?" The lawyer just billed and basically lied. You have to understand, when someone dies, and in this case, he was relatively young, only 59, there was nothing to distribute. Whatever he had was going to his wife. The only proceeding or actual settlement of the probate estate is when the last parent dies and all of the children are going to inherit their assets.

Usually, that's when a probate attorney is really useful. He just took their money, and I remember thinking that no one liked this guy and I had one reason why I didn't – he was a thief. I don't know what ever happened to him because he became a lawyer before they really started to clamp down on attorneys with ethics rules and things like that. Up until then, no one was really making lawyers accountable to their clients. Now, Connecticut does random audits on lawyers to make sure that everything is in order.

I would never do that to a client. That will be one thing that will get you disbarred. Taking serious amounts of money from clients is not only a violation of trust, but it can affect your future career. Unfortunately, some lawyers end up doing this. I know a lawyer, an older guy, who got disbarred this way. He got divorced and had to pay alimony to his wife, so he started taking money from clients. He was taking money and it was not being handled properly.

It surprised me so much because this guy had been a lawyer for about 40 years and suddenly, at the end of his career, he was actively screwing up because he felt pressured to keep up the appearance of being a successful lawyer and maintain a certain lifestyle. When lawyers get desperate enough, they will make decisions that can hurt their careers, especially when it comes to money.

When you practice law, business ebbs and flows. Some days I'm extremely busy and other days not so much. During slower times, keep busy, spend time on marketing and trying to get your name out there. Don't be desperate for clients, but make sure that you are available. I always return every call as soon as possible. That is something that I was trained to do in the very beginning of my lawyering days. Return every call the day you get it, and I go a step further and return every call the minute I know I need to.

This establishes my credibility because my clients know that I'm going to call them right back. Even if I didn't answer the phone when they called me, they know I'm calling them within the next couple hours, or as soon as I get out of court. Your clients have to be able to depend on you and it's important that they do.

In this business, you need to get comfortable having difficult and unpleasant conversations. Whether it's about money, personal life, their kids, or other things, you have to get used to that. It's your job as a lawyer to establish trust with your client.

To make sure that you are maintaining your credibility with your clients, make sure that you don't ever misrepresent anything. Don't sugarcoat things or say that you know something when you really don't. There is nothing wrong with telling a client, "You know, I don't have the answer to that right now, but I will get you the answer."

People will respect that, nobody expects you to be perfect, just make sure that you're not answering questions that you're not 100% sure about. People call with situations that you haven't come across, even if you've been a lawyer for many years. This also happens when lawyers decide to take on a new area of practice, trying something new in addition to what they're already doing.

If someone throws something at you that you're not sure about, get on the phone with other lawyers and say, "Hey, what do you know about this?" But never tell a client you have the answer if you don't. If you have the answer, great, but don't tell somebody, "Oh, this is what's going to happen," and then you're wrong.

Always remember that they're probably talking to three to five other lawyers at the same time. When they're searching for a lawyer, they get online and a number of people pop up. So, they usually end up calling and talking to different attorneys. They're getting different advice and comparing what the other attorneys have said, so you don't want to give them inaccurate information.

As you build your practice, you build your credibility. It takes years, but once you establish a rapport with clients, you'll be able to find out which areas you're well-versed in and certain areas that may need more research. There are certain situations that don't come with a manual.

There's no exact science to practicing certain areas of law. Anything financial is pretty cut and dry. As a tax attorney, you need to know your stuff, and that comes down to income, deductions, and those sorts of things. As a criminal lawyer, or a personal injury or divorce attorney, it's always a learning curve.

I believe that no matter how long you've been practicing, you are always learning how to do your job better. One of the funniest things I ever heard somebody say happened in court. The courtroom was full of attorneys, the first two rows were all lawyers. I was sitting in the front row and an older man was sitting behind me, he was probably in his seventies.

As he's sitting there talking, another guy says to him, "Oh wow. You're still at it huh?" And the lawyer replied, "Well yeah. We call it practice because we never really get good at it, we just keep trying." That really is true. Even if certain areas of law did come with a manual, laws always change.

It's impossible to know about every law when it changes, but if you are upfront about your knowledge, people will trust your decisions and know that you'll take whatever steps necessary to give them what they need.

Chapter 11.

Marketing Yourself

Marketing yourself is a vital part of maintaining a successful practice. Not only is it a way to get your name out there, it establishes credibility. Marketing on your own is vastly different from marketing for somebody else, such as a firm. In Connecticut, you must be a lawyer in order to market for that specific law firm. You can hire an online marketing company because it's not face-to-face marketing, but if you want to market in-house, you have to find a lawyer to do it.

Marketing for an established firm can sometimes be easier due to name recognition. When you market for a firm, you market the entire team, not individual attorneys. In big firms, the marketing, to me, is very stiff, because they're appealing to corporations and big shot clients.

Most people who need a lawyer don't need a big-shot lawyer. They need somebody who's going to listen to them and help them solve their problem. For my practice, I am the lawyer and I market myself. People are hiring me, not a firm, so I am the product. You have to find ways to stand out because, if you don't work at a big, established, law firm, you won't have their resources. Most lawyers don't fall into that category. Most attorneys decide to open an office with a couple friends from law school or end up going to work at a smaller office that is less well-known.

As the product, you need to present yourself so that people take you seriously. You are a walking advertisement, and if you walk around wearing jeans every day, you're not going to get hired by people. If you're that casual about your business, you won't have any business to speak of. As you build your practice, constantly think of ways to improve your marketing efforts.

If you're working at a firm, get together with your partners and put a plan in place. This is the one area of law practice that can either make you stand out or get lost among your peers.

I love marketing, even though it's very frustrating. The frustration comes from not knowing if something is going to work until you try it. Then, even if it works, you could try that same approach in a couple years and it might not work. When it comes to marketing, what works today is not necessarily going to work tomorrow.

When people are looking for legal help, they're not finding lawyers the same way they were 20 years ago. Twenty years ago, you heard about lawyers through friends, acquaintances, or you went through the yellow pages. A lawyer had a decent little ad and they could have a pretty good practice. With the internet, now you have the entire world at your fingertips. If somebody needs a certain type of lawyer, all they have to do is go in and type their city followed by the type of lawyer they need.

You have to stay on top of how people are finding attorneys, and if you don't have client reviews and peer reviews by other attorneys, you're probably not going to get hired unless you have a really great website. I have been hired by people who would compliment my website. They didn't know anything else about me, they would just say, "Wow, you have a really great website. I really want to work with you. I hope this is going to work out." After they talked to me, I was hired, and it did work out.

As a lawyer, you've got to be careful with marketing because companies are always going to think that you're rolling in money. There's a handful of lawyers that are, and they're usually personal injury lawyers, because they're always the dominant ones in every market, but they are not in the majority. If it's personal injury, they usually spend massive amounts of money on advertising, billboards, television commercials, and more.

You can access that type of marketing if you have that kind of money, but if you don't, you've got to find other ways of getting your name out there. For most people, that takes time. You really have to be patient and focus on the image that you want to put out there. There are a couple of lawyers that advertise in the market where I live. They seem trustworthy and use a catchy slogan, but they have since changed their marketing strategy.

In their first commercials, they both wore suits and ties. In the second set, they're seen sitting in a restaurant with their top button unbuttoned. No tie or jacket. They went from polished looking attorneys to casual attorneys, obviously as an effort to appeal to a potentially wider audience.

Sometimes when people are looking for attorneys, they don't have time to find the best lawyer. If you had a wrongful death in the family, are you going to focus on what the attorneys are wearing in the commercial? No. You're going to ask your friends or family members to help you find a lawyer, and chances are, they're going to pick the one whom they've seen advertised.

In your marketing efforts, it's important for you to know what image you're putting out there and who your target client is. To find out how to appeal to these people, ask yourself some questions. Why is this person your ideal client? Why do you want this person as a client? What things are they going to be looking for when they hire a lawyer? You'll figure it out, and then it will change.

That's what makes marketing so frustrating. A lot of lawyers don't like doing it because it just changes and changes and changes. To be successful, you've got to adjust to those changes. You can't view it as a hassle or a pain. Marketing can be really fun when you look at the benefits of it.

Put your mind to it and figure out what you want to say about yourself. How do I want to come across to people so that they will want to work with me and hire me? These are questions that only you can answer. Or, if you're working at a firm, your team of lawyers can get together and brainstorm ideas.

A major part of your marketing efforts has to do with visibility. How does your marketing portray how you are going to help your clients? This is the opportunity to tell people who you are. Don't be shy; push yourself. I knew a lawyer in my town who got disbarred. He was smart, brilliant, and one of the nicest people I knew. As nice as he was, he was a little overzealous.

There was a big fire in my town. The fire burned down a factory which was surrounded by residential homes. He figured out that because of this big fire, which had occurred at a chemical company, people in the area must have gotten sick. He had no proof of this whatsoever, but he just started to go around the neighborhood knocking on doors. He introduced himself as a personal injury lawyer and told residents that he wanted to represent them in a class action suit against the company where this fire had taken place.

These people were regular people who didn't know what else to say so they agreed. He asked if family members had gotten sick and nobody confirmed that, so he waited a couple months and went out again. This time, he got into a lot of trouble. You can't do that. You can't go to people and recruit them to be part of a lawsuit, they have to come to you. There's a right and wrong way to advertise yourself – this was a bad one. There are class action lawsuits now, but most firms advertise it to the public at large, they don't knock on doors.

Bottom-line, don't have a bad attitude about marketing. If you do, change it. Otherwise your phone will never ring, and no one will ever know who you are. Learn more about marketing, look into announcements, or radio advertising. It's not very expensive and it will improve your business.

Chapter 12.

Being a Lawyer (It's a Business)

The main difference between lawyers and business is money. In a business, the focus is money. It's about making the most and having the best. As soon as a new invention comes out, what happens shortly after? All the competitors copy it. I have seen this over and over again.

A friend of mine sells a clothing line and I buy clothes from her. I remember the first time I heard the term 'boyfriend jeans', all the sudden, everyone was using that term. Every single clothing company out there started using the term boyfriend jeans and I thought, "It would be really annoying to be the person that coined this term and all of the sudden people are just using your little phrase all over the world."

Businesses focus on money, profits, and sales. As a lawyer, the motivation is different, but the approach is the same. One thing about being an attorney is that you can, and you should, look to other attorneys for guidance, information, and a sense of belonging. You should never feel like you're alone in everything you do.

Not only do you need lawyer friends, but you should have a list of other attorneys that you learn from.

Find lawyers who write books or who are well known out there in the current world. You can also find books written by attorneys who are no longer with us. Learn from their life experiences.

There was a very well-known criminal defense attorney who was known for being a slob. His hair always looked kind of messy and his clothes were never ironed or neat. But, he was a great lawyer. He was always busy, always working, because it was his life. As a lawyer, you can't just have money be your focus, but you have to make money and get paid. Being an attorney is also your profession and you should put value on what you do.

Is it important to understand how you are going to be compensated and how that number was determined. If you're a government employee, what you're going to make is determined between you and your supervisor. But if you're on your own, or you work with a firm, know what you're getting paid.

Financial details vary from practice to practice. Your income is going to be different if you joined a firm as somebody who's going to help bring in business or if you started up a firm with a couple friends from law school. You always have to keep the money in mind, but it shouldn't be the main concern.

There were five lawyers I knew, and their main focus was money. You know what? They're not lawyers anymore. They either ended up in jail, out of a practice, or both. So, going to jail may not be the end of the world, you'll possibly still have your license. But if you put money ahead of people in your law practice, not only do you not understand what being a lawyer is all about, but you also don't understand that you could be breaking the law and find yourself in hot water.

The difference between us and businesses is that it's not the only concern that we get to have. Our main priority is being the best lawyer we can be, every single day. As a lawyer, you have to put people before profits.

Aside from money, it is important to consider ethics. To me, if you want to be a good lawyer, you have to treat everyone the same. In this business, you should always treat everyone you come across with respect and kindness. I treat prosecutors the same way that I treat the clerks that I don't really have that much contact with. I just try to be nice to everyone and not categorize people that I run into by how much they can do for me. Just be yourself, but be yourself with everyone.

Whether you like it or not, you are a product. As a lawyer, you're out in the community, you never know who you're going to come across. You never know where your next referral is going to come from. If you don't treat people well, you won't get anywhere. Other lawyers won't want to work with you or send you cases. It will affect your reputation, and you won't make it. As I've said before, this is a people business. In the business of lawyering, being a respectful, warm, approachable person is one of the things you have to try to master.

There was a lawyer I tried to go work for, probably 15 years ago. I'm a very fast learner and I'm a very responsible person. I'm good at figuring out what I need to do as an attorney and I'm confident in that. I got on the phone with this guy and, because I wasn't a highly experienced attorney, he acted like I was wasting his time. He was so unkind to me on the phone and I have never forgotten that about him. I have always just thought of him as somebody I didn't need to know, and I would never help him out.

At the time, I was in a place where I wanted to come work for him. Instead of treating me with kindness, he was dismissive. It left an impression and I would never dream of treating anybody that way. Everyone you meet has value.

To prioritize your practice, look into continuing education. There are so many associations for lawyers. The state Bar is in all fifty states, and in the federal system, the opportunities for education are endless. If you don't engage in them, you're not staying on top of what you do.

As a lawyer, it's important to stay on top of the laws and know when they change and how they change. Pay attention to the little things. One day I was in the judge's chambers when me, him, and a prosecutor are talking. I tell the prosecutor that the reason I don't think you can find my guy guilty of a DUI is because he was not on the road. He was in his yard and he stayed in his yard until he moved his truck out of the garage and hit the neighbor's fence.

After I said this, he told me that they removed the requirement from the statute. Meaning that you can be charged with a DUI from anywhere, even if you're not on the road. The judge didn't even know about the change, which doesn't happen often. Most judges know a lot more about things than they ever let on, but because they're judges, they're usually kind of quiet. They usually just act as a referee.

This reminded me how important it is to be on top of changes in the law. As you go along, always learn as much as you can. Sometimes that involves taking classes or talking to other lawyers. One thing you should always remember is to never be afraid of a particular outcome. It took me a while to get to this point, but you eventually realize that it's not your outcome. If you have done the best that you can for whoever you happen to be working for, a business client, personal client, or a corporation, it's because you were paying attention to your area or areas that you practice in.

You'll be a better lawyer if you keep on learning. Keep taking seminars and look for programs in your area. In Connecticut, and most states, they require twelve hours of continuing education every year. This is a new requirement that started last year, but most states have certain requirements, and you should know what they are. And you should be able to show that you complied with them. Nobody should have to be told about this.

When Connecticut came out with these twelve hours of continuing education, some of my friends were annoyed by it. I didn't care because I'm always taking seminars. I do at least twelve hours every year, but I bet I do a lot more than that. The bottom line is, if you're not interested in what you're doing, you're probably not in the right field.

Chapter 13.

Living the Life

There are a lot of common misconceptions about success. Society has convinced us that to be successful you have to work non-stop, never take a day off, and push yourself to the top. The truth is, success is a combination of effective practices and good decisions. You have to balance your life in order to be successful.

So take those vacations, get away, get better. I know attorneys who think that if they just don't take a vacation, if they just work a little longer, then they'll make it. If you're actively making that decision, it's not going to happen. I hardly know any lawyers who can take more than one week off at a time, myself included. If it's feasible to travel and take a vacation, find a way to take a shorter break to recharge.

The lawyers I know who can actually take three-month vacations are people have been doing this for years and who are really successful. The few other lawyers that I know who do take regular vacations are still working. They'll go somewhere for a period of time, like Bermuda or Italy, and still take calls and get work done. They never seem to stop, and it is hard to put the phone down and put the computer away, but you have to find balance.

Part of being a successful lawyer includes taking care of yourself. Don't ignore your health. I know lawyers who have ignored their health and they really regretted it. Watch your diet, watch your weight. You've got to be careful to eat healthfully and not to drink too much. If you have high blood pressure, take your medication. Whatever it is, take care of yourself. As you get older, you're going to develop certain health issues. It's the natural progression of things, so do what you can to prioritize your health.

Some things you can't avoid, but make sure that you don't ignore them. There are lawyers out there who start making money and start gaining weight. They're having fun because they're going out to all these great dinners and going on expensive vacations, but they forget to take care of their bodies. Your body is your tool. You don't want to be the lawyer who can't show up to court because you're hungover. You won't last very long as an attorney. You have to care about yourself and your body.

Through the years, I've known lawyers who end up having a practice but never really being successful. They end up not putting care into their personal appearance and it affects their business. They don't like what they do, but they don't know how to get out of it. Having balance means getting out of bed every day and being able to put a smile on your face. Studies show that attorneys are not happy people. While I do know some who aren't, I also know plenty who are. The happy attorneys are the ones who know when to put the work down and drop it for the rest of the day.

When clients text me on a Sunday, I don't text them back. Whatever the issue may be, I don't respond because my brain is shut off during that time. You have to reach that point and know when that point is. You can't do this when you're a brand-new attorney because, when you start out, it's what you're living for, but you can't run at full speed forever.

I knew a girl out of law school who was on law review. We went to the same schools and she was always an honor student. She graduated with the highest honors out of college and graduated top of her class from law school. She got a job in New York City making great money. This was 1989 and her starting salary was $90,000, which at the time, was a very good starting pay, even in New York City.

She was working at a big firm and all she did was work. I remember when I saw her in the courthouse I was working at, she told me that New York hadn't really worked out and that she had quit that job after about nine months. She got out of law school and ended working over 100 hours a week. I don't even know how that's possible, but she told me that she worked every day from 6:00 am to midnight. She would go home, crawl into bed, and get out of bed at 5:00 am, with just enough time to shower and walk out the door.

The building she was living in was full of other young professionals. People working on Wall Street, law firms, whatever it was. She said that in that building, they averaged one suicide a month. These were people just like her. Great students, intelligent, ambitious, and coming from all kinds of backgrounds. The thing was, they were all getting beaten up every day going to work and having no life.

You can stomach that for a while if you're young enough and ambitious enough to tough it out. A couple years at the most. What really pushed her to leave was when a friend came to visit for the weekend. She had already planned to have all of her work done so that she could spend time with her friend. Then, her boss comes into her and says, "I need this brief by Monday morning." She was devastated because she had made plans with her friend.

Despite her best efforts at time management and efficiency, she did not get to spend any time with her friend. Her friend ended up touring New York City by herself all weekend as she got the brief done. She goes to his office 7:30 Monday morning and hands him the brief. Turns out, he didn't need it that morning after all. She looked at him and said, "I'm leaving. I'm done." She went to her office, cleaned out her desk, and left.

Everybody in that firm went to great schools all over the country. They were all there pursuing their careers, yet nobody was happy and everybody was always working. If that's not something that appeals to you, you've got to find the right firm to work with. A lot of firms are going to try to get you to join by telling you how great it's going to be, but you're always going to work more hours than your employer told you that you were going to work. That just comes with the territory, especially in the first five years.

Even now, as long as I've been a lawyer, which is 25 years, there are times that I still work more than I want to be working. But you know what? It comes with the territory. People I know who have done 30, 40, 50, and even 100 trials tell me that no matter how many trials they do, they still don't sleep when they're doing a trial. Here they are, some of them in their sixties, and they're telling me that they still don't get sleep.

This is not a nine to five job, you have to know when to work and when to stop. This is a difficult business to stay positive in because we're constantly dealing with people's problems. That's what we do. It can be a heavy burden, and you have to deal with it. But you should find some way to live a happy life in spite of that.

Go have fun with your kids or husband. Meet your girlfriends for dinner, go on a date, whatever it is, find a way to get away from work. Even if you just go hang out by yourself at a park or at the beach, find what is going to bring you peace so that you can re-group. You have to find that time because if you don't, you will burn out and end up hating what you do. You will not make it. There is a five-year recidivism rate with a lot of attorneys. They get out, and they start practicing, and they just become consumed by it.

A lot of times when that happens, I think it means that they didn't pick the right area of law to go into to. They end up getting beat up and they just decide to stop doing it. They leave the profession, but they never really find out who they are. Even if they do stay in the field, success usually doesn't look like they anticipated it would. Truth is, you're only as good as your last case. Even if you never sleep and don't have a life outside of work. It's not going to make you a better attorney, just an overworked one.

Nowadays especially, I think people are afraid to make mistakes, or at least admit them, but they are going to happen. You have to be able to recover and learn not to do that again. There's always going to be times when you wish you had done something different; learn from those mistakes.

Part of learning from mistakes is knowing what moves to make. Don't be desperate. There's always going to be cases that you want to take, but you're unsure about. Be able to recognize a good case and a bad case. I don't work for a firm, but I won't take a case because another lawyer has had the file too long or I'm not going to be able to undo what's already been done. When a case gets to a certain age, it is what it is. It takes time. In the beginning, you're not going to be able to spot the bad cases, but as time goes on, you will. You're going to get some bad cases no matter what, that's just the way it is. Every once in awhile I'll end up with a case and think to myself, "How did I end up with this?" But you've just got to move forward and plow through it. That's it.

Being a lawyer offers a lot of opportunities, but there are also situations that are not beneficial from a professional aspect. A friend of mine used to approach me to see if I could work for this corporation–he was their Massachusetts counsel. He said, "They're looking for counsel for Connecticut, are you interested?" Right off the bat I said, "No. "

He was surprised by my answer and questioned why I would not even consider the position. The reason for this was because corporations will always treat you like you are a dime a dozen. Although there are some corporate attorneys out there who are very happy, most companies hire a handful of attorneys and you are not valued as an individual. Value yourself and know your worth; don't work for people who don't care about you.

Building your practice takes time, years. It won't happen overnight, it's a day-to-day process. If you get through the first five years, you're at the beginning of viewing yourself as a lawyer. If you get through the next five years, then you've reached the point where you're a lawyer. If you think that by making it two years into a job, that you're a lawyer, you're wrong. You're not really a lawyer until you've been doing it for 10 years, because a lot of attorneys don't make it for that first five years. Once you make it past that, after 10 years, you're not going anywhere.

After that point, what else are you going to do with your life? If you last that long, it means that you love it enough, or at least you like it enough. You're successful enough to keep doing it and you just have to know what you're about. Sometimes I wonder what else I would be doing if I wasn't a lawyer, and honestly, I'm not sure. If someone told me I had to find something else to do, once I got over the devastation of that, I'd probably go into sales. That's what a lot of lawyers do when they change careers, because we're good at talking and convincing people of things.

But that's the thing, I really wouldn't want to be doing anything else. One of the things I tell people about being a lawyer is to be what you want to be. Be the kind of lawyer you want to be. Don't say that you want to be a lawyer and then find yourself in an area of law that you don't like. If it's boring to you, find a different one. Areas of the law that I could never do are bankruptcy, or probate. A probate lawyer tried to get me into doing probate and I just couldn't be convinced. I remember seeing him with a calculator and pencil always adding things and doing math and I knew it just wasn't for me.

I love what I do, and I believe that people should be a lover first, fighter second. If you start out fighting, forget it. You're going to end up with an ulcer, or a heart attack. You will be extremely unhappy. If you get known as a fighter in this business, people are not going to want to deal with you. It doesn't matter what gender you are, if you get known as a fighter, you're probably not going to have a career and you may end up being very unhappy. I say probably because there are some people who are natural-born fighters, but there's not many of them.

It's okay to be hungry, but don't be too serious or overly aggressive. Just like in sports, there is always one person on every team who is too aggressive. I played varsity soccer in high school and sure enough, instead of tackling the ball, the aggressive player would tackle the person. They would end up hurting the person because they didn't seem to grasp that they were supposed to be going after the ball, not the person.

There are lawyers who are the exact same way. They don't grasp that you're not supposed to go after the lawyer on the other side of the table. You've got to keep the prize in mind, remember that you're going after the ball. The ball is the problem and you have to try to solve the problem.

Nobody is going to give it to you. You have to take it. Think to yourself, "If I could be any lawyer, in my wildest dreams I would be …", and become it.

About the Author

Connecticut attorney Erin M. Field has been fighting for the rights of her clients for more than two decades. After graduating from the Western New England College School of Law, Erin founded her own law practice in 1992. Through her practice, Erin has helped numerous Connecticut residents with a variety of legal problems. She works hard to deliver excellent service to each of her clients, and uses her skills and experience to get the best possible results in each case.

Erin is a member of the Connecticut Bar Association, the Connecticut Trial Lawyers Association, the Connecticut Criminal Defense Lawyers Association, the Hartford County Bar Association, and the Personal Injury Lawyers Marketing and Management Association.

In every case she takes, Erin provides excellent, thorough, and accessible service. Erin is an effective negotiator and vigorous litigator. She takes time to clearly explain the law and the legal process to each of her clients. Erin understands that each of her cases and clients are unique. That is why she offers personal and accessible service, always giving each case the individualized attention that it deserves.

Practice Areas

Attorney Erin M. Field is qualified to handle a variety of legal matters in the State of Connecticut, but her practice has focused on personal injury, criminal defense, and DUI/DWI defense.

- Personal injury. If you have been injured due to the wrongful conduct of someone else, you are entitled to compensation for your harm. Attorney Erin M. Field fights for justice for personal injury victims in Connecticut.

- Criminal defense. Criminal convictions can bring severe consequences. Every person charged with a crime in Connecticut deserves an effective defense and has a right to a fair trial. If you've been charged with a crime in Connecticut, attorney Erin M. Field can investigate the facts of your case to identify all possible defenses, protect your substantive and procedural rights, negotiate with the prosecution, and if necessary vigorously represent you at trial.

- DUI/DWI defense. In many cases, there are legitimate defenses to DUI/DWI charges. In other cases, the punishment can be minimized. Whatever the facts of the case, attorney Erin M. Field helps those charged with DUI/DWI get the best possible outcome in a cost-effective way.

www.ingramcontent.com/pod-product-compliance
Lightning Source LLC
Chambersburg PA
CBHW071104210326
41519CB00020B/6164